P I A S:
SUPERNATURAL SESSIONS

By Barbara A. Perry

GARDEN 33 PUBLISHER
P. O. BOX 197
Aiken, S.C. 29802

POWER IN ACTION SESSIONS
By Barbara A. Perry

Copyright © 2013 Barbara A. Perry

ISBN 978-0-9960442-1-9

Unless otherwise noted, Scriptures quotations are from the King James Version of the Bible.
Copyright © 1989 Thomas Nelson, Inc., publishers.

ALL RIGHTS RESERVED.

NO PART OF THIS BOOK MAY BE REPRODUCED IN ANY FORM, BY PHOTOCOPING OR BY ANY ELECTRONIC OR MECHANICAL MEANS, INCLUDING INFORMATION STORAGE OR RETRIEVAL SYSTEMS, WITHOUT PERMISSION IN WRITING FROM THE COPYRIGHT OWNER/AUTHOR.

Printed in the U.S.A.

Garden 33 Publisher
P. O. Box 197
Aiken, S.C. 29802

Thanks to the faithful members of
Spirit Of Prevailing Faith for their anticipation,
participation, and support in these sessions!

TABLE OF CONTENT

	Page
Introduction	6
The Believer's Weapons	8
Session 1 Taking Thoughts Captive	14
Session 2 Casting Down Imaginations	20
Session 3 Pulling Down/Demolishing Strongholds	23
Session 4A Casting Out Demons	28
Session 4B Spiritual Authority	30
Session 5 The Suppressor of Light	36
Session 6A The Power of Faith	39
Session 6B Greater Works/Created Miracles	41
Prayer Combined With Ways To Heal	45

INTRODUCTION

PIA sessions are designed to aid the Believers in releasing the power within. PIAS will provide you the opportunity to advance over the obstacles in the flesh through actual action exercises. PIAS will instill in you the confidence and boldness you need to face the enemy and minister healing and deliverance to others and yourself. It's design to heighten your expectation for miracles, signs, and wonders. PIAS are not sessions for operating in the Gifts of the Spirits (I Corinthians 12:4-11) PIAS can be used individually or as a group. In these sessions the Believer will be:

- Exercising: Faith
- Exercising: Authority over demons
- Exercising: Greater works activities

In **Mark 16:13**-18 it is written, "He said to them, "Go into all the world and preach the good news to all creation. Whoever believes and is baptized will be saved, but whoever does not believe will be condemned. And these signs will accompany those who believe: In my name they will drive out demons; they will speak in new tongues; they will pick up snakes with their hands; and when they drink deadly poison, it will not hurt them at all; they will place their hands on sick people, and they will get well."

> Jesus said these signs will accompany those who believe: If you are not a Believer, but desire to become a Believer, please pray this prayer: Lord, I am a sinner. Please forgive me of my sins. Come into my heart and live your life through me. I receive you as my Saviour and Lord. Jesus fill me with the Holy Spirit, that I may have your power to live life as a Christian. Thank you, Lord. Amen.

Mark 11:22-24 *"Have faith in God,"* Jesus answered. I tell you the truth, if anyone says to this mountain, 'Go throw yourself into the sea,' and does not doubt in his heart but believes that what he says will happen; it will be done for him. Therefore I tell you, whatever you ask for in prayer, believe that you have received it, and it will be yours."

Luke 10:19 "Behold, I give unto you power to tread on serpents and scorpions, and over all the power of the enemy; and nothing shall by any means hurt you."

The Believer's Weapons:

Our weapons are mighty because they are spiritually divine.

> Weapons are available for every Believer. Below is a list of weapons with related Scriptures. [See Ephesians 6:10-18] We are instructed to put on the whole armor of God.

Jesus' Name   Prayer   Faith

Authority   Fasting   Meditating on the Word

Praise & Worship   The Word (Confessing/Speaking)

Imagination/visualize

Scriptures that relate to our weapons:

Jesus' name

^{23} "And in that day ye shall ask me nothing. Verily, verily, I say unto you, Whatsoever ye shall ask the father in my name, he will give it you. ^{24} Hitherto have ye asked nothing <u>in my name:</u> ask, and ye shall receive, that your joy may be full." **John 16:23,24**

Additions scriptures: John 14:13,14; John 15:16; Mark 16:17; Phil. 2:9,10

Prayer

"And in that day ye shall ask me nothing. Verily, verily, I say unto you, Whatsoever ye shall ask the father in my name, he will give it you. ^{24} Hitherto have ye asked nothing in my name: <u>ask,</u> and ye shall receive, that your joy may be full." **John 16:23,24**

"Be careful (anxious) for nothing; but in every thing <u>by prayer</u> and supplication with thanksgiving let your requests be made known unto God. ^{7} And the peace of God, which passeth all understanding, shall keep your hearts and minds through Christ Jesus." **Phil. 4:6,7**

Additional scriptures: Mark 11:24; James 4:2; I John 5:14,15

Faith

"***Have faith in God***," Jesus answered. I tell you the truth, if anyone says to this mountain, 'Go throw yourself into the sea,' and does not doubt in his heart but believes that what he says will happen; it will be done for him. Therefore I tell you, whatever you ask for in prayer, believe that you have received it, and it will be yours." **Mark 11:22-24**

"And Jesus said unto them, Because of your unbelief: for verily I say unto you, If ye have faith as a grain of mustard seed, ye shall say unto this mountain, Remove hence to yonder place; and it shall remove (move); and nothing shall be impossible unto you." **Matt. 17:20**

"But without faith it is impossible to please him: for he that cometh to God must believe that he is, and that he is a rewarder of them that diligently seek him." **Heb. 11:6**

Additional scriptures: Matt. 21: 20-22; Luke 17:6; James 2:26

Authority

authority – 2 **a :** power to influence or command thought, opinion, or behavior

<u>re: the devil and his demons:</u> You do not have to allow them to beat up on you. As a child of God and his Spirit that dwells in you, – through the power of Jesus' name and Spirit – you can take authority of his weapons.

[19] "Behold, I give unto you power to tread on serpents and scorpions, and over all the power of the enemy; and nothing shall by any means hurt you." [20] Notwithstanding in this rejoice not, that the spirits are subject unto you: but rather rejoice, because your names are written in heaven." **Luke 10:19,20**

"And hath raised us up together, and made us sit together in heavenly places in Christ Jesus." **Ephesians 2: 6**

[15] "For ye have not received the spirit of bondage again to fear; but ye have received the Spirit of adoption, whereby we cry, Abba, Father. [16] The Spirit itself beareth witness with our spirit, that we are the children of God: [17] **And if children, then heirs; heirs of God, and joint-heirs with Christ**; if so be that we suffer with him, that we may be also glorified together." **Romans 8:15 – 17**

"Ye are of God, little children, and have overcome them: because greater is he that is in you, than he that is in the world." **I John 4:4**

Additions scriptures: 2 Corinthians 10:3-5; Eph. 6:10-18; Col. 1:12-13; Isaiah 54:15-17

Fasting

[16] "Moreover when ye fast, be not, as the hypocrites, of a sad countenance: for they disfigure their faces, that they may appear unto men to fast. Verily I say unto you, They have their reward. [17] But thou, when thou fastest, anoint thine head, and wash thy face; [18] That thou appear not unto men to fast, but unto thy Father which is in secret: and thy Father, which seeth in secret, shall reward thee openly." **Matt. 6:16-18**

"Howbeit this kind goeth not out but by prayer and fasting." **Matt. 17:21**

Additional scriptures: **Isaiah 58 chapter.**

Praise
{Magnify and adore Him}

praise n - **1 a :** an expression of approval : COMMENDATION **b :** WORSHIP **2 a :** VALUE, MERIT

praise vb **praised; praising** – **1 :** to express a favorable judgment of : COMMEND **2 :** to glorify (a god or saint) esp. by the attribution of perfections ~ vi : to express praise.

"But thou art holy, O thou that inhabitest the praises of Israel." **Psalm 22:3**

[21]"And when he had consulted with the people, he appointed singers unto the LORD, and that should praise the beauty of holiness, as they went out before the army, and to say, Praise the LORD; for his mercy endureth for ever. [22] And when they began to sing and to praise, the LORD set ambushments against the children of Ammon, Moab, and mount Seir, which were come against Judah; and they were smitten." **2 Chronicles 20:21,22**

Additional scriptures: Psalm 149 chapter; John 12:32

Worship
{Acknowledge God for who He is}

worship vb -shipped, -shipping – **1 :** to honor or reverence as a divine being or supernatural power **2 :** to regard with great, even extravagant respect, honor or devotion

worship – to make obeisance, do reverence to. to serve.

Worship is deeper than praise. It causes you to bow before God.

"O come, let us worship and bow down: let us kneel before the LORD our maker." **Psalm 95:6**

"O worship the LORD in the beauty of holiness; fear (tremble) before him, all the earth." **Psalm 96:9**

"Give unto the LORD the glory due unto his name: bring an offering, and come before him: worship the LORD in the beauty of holiness." **I Chronicles 16:29**

Imagination/Visualization

"Where there is no vision the people perish:" Prov. 29:18a
"For as he thinketh in his heart, so is he:" Prov. 23:7a

imagination – **1:** the act or power of forming a mental image of something not present to the senses never before wholly perceived in reality **2 : a** creative ability **3 a** : a creation of the mind; *esp* : an idealized or poetic creation **b** : fanciful or empty assumption

visualization – 1 : formation of mental visual images.

transcendental meditation – a technique of meditation in which a mantra is chanted in order to foster calm, creativity, and spiritual well-being.

mantra – a mystical formula of invocation or incantation (as in Hinduism)

Imagination can be used for good or evil. Do not form mental images in your mind and use mantra; such as, transcendental meditation.

Speaking the WORD

"Have faith in God," Jesus answered. I tell you the truth, if anyone says to this mountain, 'Go throw yourself into the sea,' and does not doubt in his heart but believes that what he says will happen; it will be done for him. Therefore I tell you, whatever you ask for in prayer, believe that you have received it, and it will be yours." **Mark 11:22-24**

"And Jesus said unto them, Because of your unbelief: for verily I say unto you, If ye have faith as a grain of mustard seed, ye shall say unto this mountain, Remove hence to yonder place; and it shall remove (move); and nothing shall be impossible unto you." **Matt. 17:20**

[20] "A man's belly shall be satisfied with the fruit of his mouth; and with the increase of his lips shall he be filled. [21] Death and life are in the power of the tongue: and they that love it shall eat the fruit thereof." **Prov. 18:20,21**

Additional scriptures: Prov. 6:2; 12:4; 12:18; 13:2

Meditating on the WORD

meditation – quiet contemplation of spiritual truths.

meditate – to engage in contemplation or reflection to focus one's thoughts on: reflect on or ponder over by talking/muttering to oneself.

[97] "Oh, how I love your law! I meditate on it all day long. [98] Thou through thy commandments hast made me wiser than mine enemies: for they are ever with me. [99] I have more insight than all my teachers, because I meditate on your status. [100] I have more understanding than the elders, for I obey your precepts." **Psalm 119:97 – 100**

[5] "My soul will be satisfied as with the richest of foods; with singing lips my mouth will praise you.
[6] On my bed I remember you; I think of you through the watches of the night." **Psalm 63:5,6**

"My eyes stay open through the watches of the night, that I may meditate on your promises." **Psalm 119:148**

Additional scriptures: Psalm 1:2,3; Psalm 119:148; Joshua 1:8

SESSION #1

Scripture Reading – I Corinthians 2:6 – 16   Wisdom From Heaven

Session & Action Exercises #1   Taking Thoughts Captive

2 Corinth. 10:3-5 "For though we walk in the flesh, we do not war after the flesh; (For the **weapons** of our warfare are not carnal, but **mighty through God** to the pulling down of strong holds;) Casting down imaginations, and every high thing that exalteth itself against the knowledge of God, and **bringing into captivity every thought to the obedience of Christ;**

……. [7] Do you look on things after the outward appearance?

The enemy does a lot of damage to individuals through the power of thought. When we have a negative, wrong, or bad thought, the enemy will enlarge it. He even drops some of them in our mind. All of them are not from the enemy, but are from the sinful nature of man. But whether they are from the sinful nature or the devil, we are instructed to take them captive.

The devil comes to steal, kill, and destroy… **(John 10:10)**. And he will work from every angle to accompany his purpose.

Healthy thinking feeds the spirit and soul. Turn your thinking around. Think on right thing and heavenly things.   **Read Phil. 4:8 and Col. 3:2**

Here are some example statements that enter our thought and Scriptures in response to them. The correct way to response to these is to follow Jesus' example: It is written. Or you can say, The Word says. ['It is written' and 'the Word said' are equivalent.]

Exercise { Read the statement out loud that you may be dealing with, then take the thought captive with the respond}

SPIRIT

Thought/Statement: It is impossible to be born again.
Respond: *It is written*, "....With men it is impossible, but not with God: for with God all things are possible." Mark 10:27

It is written, "But as many as received him, to them gave he power to become the sons of God, even to them that believe on his name:" John 1:12

Thought/Statement: You are not born again.
It is *written*, "But as many as received him, to them gave he power to become the sons of God, even to them that believe on his name:" John 1:12

Respond: *It is written*, "Therefore if any man be in Christ, he is a new creature: old things are passed away; behold, all things are become new." 2 Corinth. 5:17

Thought/Statement: You are not a child of God or you are nobody.
Respond: *It is written*, "But as many as received him, to them gave he power to become the sons of God, even to them that believe on his name:" John 1:12

Read Romans 8:14 - 17

SOUL

You are a spirit being placed in a physical body with a Soul. Your soul consists of :
A Mind [intellect]
A Will [choice, attitude, self-control]
Emotion [feelings]

God's will is for your soul to prosper:
"Beloved, I wish above all things that thou mayest prosper and be in health, even as though soul prospereth." III John 2

"If any of you lack wisdom, let him ask of God, that giveth to all men liberally, and upbraideth not; and it shall be given him." James 1:5

Thought/Statement: You will never amount to anything you are too weak.

Response: *It is written*, "And hath made us kings and priests unto God and his Father, to him be glory and dominion for ever and ever. Amen." Rev. 1:6

[29] "He giveth power to the faint(weak); and to them that have no might he increaseth strength. .... [31] But they that wait upon the LORD shall renew their strength; they shall mount up with wings as eagles; they shall run, and not be weary; and they shall walk, and not faint." Isaiah 40:29 ,31

It is written, "Greater is He that is in me than he that is in the world." I John 4:4
It is written, " I am more than a conquer." Rom. 8:37

Also I John 5:4,5

It is written, "The LORD is my shepherd; I shall not want (lack). He restoreth my soul: he leadeth me in the paths of righteousness for his name's sake."   Ps. 23:1,3

It is written, " The LORD is my light and my salvation; whom shall I fear? The LORD is the strength of my life; of whom shall I be afraid?" Psalm 27:1

It is written, "I will love thee, O LORD my strength." Psalm 18:1

God has a good plan for your life:
It is written, "For I know the thoughts that I think toward you, saith the LORD, thoughts of peace, and not of evil, to give you an expected end (a future and a hope)." Jeremiah 29:11

Godly wisdom will deliver and keep you from destruction of self and wicked people:
[10] " When wisdom entereth into thine heart, and knowledge is pleasant unto thy soul; [11] Discretion shall preserve thee, understanding shall keep thee: [12] to deliver thee from the way of the evil man, from the man that speaketh forward (perverse) things." Prov. 2;10-12

BODY

Thought/Statement: God has not made provision for your physical healing?
Response: *It is written*, [4] "Surely he hath borne our griefs (sicknesses), and carried our sorrows (pains): yet we did esteem his stricken, smitten of God, and afflicted. [5] But he was wounded for our transgression, he was bruised for our iniquities: the chastisement of our peace was upon him; and with his stripes we are healed." Isaiah 53:4,5

Though/Statement: There's no medicine or cure for this infirmity.
Response: *It is written*, "He sent his word, and healed them, and delivered them from their destructions." Psalm 107:20

It is written, [20] "My son, attend to my words;... [22] For they are life unto those that find them, and health to all their flesh." Prov. 4:20.22

It is written, "But if the Spirit of him that raised up Jesus from the dead dwell in you, he that raised up Christ from the dead shall also quicken (give life to) your mortal bodies by his Spirit that dwelleth in you (or because of) his Spirit that dwelleth in you." Roms. 8:11

FINANCES

Statement/Thought: A Christian was meant to live in poverty. God does not want you to have money. God does not care about your financial well-being or about meeting your needs. Black people are supposed to be poor and the white are supposed to be rich. God had cursed the black and blessed the white.

Response: *It is written,* "For there is no respect of persons with God." Romans 2:11

Psalm 23:1 "The LORD is my shepherd; I shall not want (lack)"

If you believe that statement, then you don't know the Word of God. Please don't be destroyed in your life and finances because of a lack of the knowledge of the Word. When we follow the principle in the Word, we will prosper. Below are some scriptures that will teach you how to receive in your life and finances.

"Will a man rob God? Yet ye have robbed me. But ye say, Wherein have we robbed thee? In tithes and offerings. ⁹ Ye are cursed with a curse: for ye have robbed me, even this whole nation. ¹⁰ Bring all the tithes into the storehouse, that there may be meat in mine house, and prove me now herewith, saith the LORD of hosts, if I will not open you the windows of heaven, and pour you out a blessing, that there shall not be room enough to receive it. ¹¹ And I will rebuke the devourer for your sakes, and he shall not destroy the fruits of your ground; neither shall your vine cast her fruit before the time in the field, saith the LORD of hosts. ¹² And all nations shall call you blessed: for ye shall be a delightsome land, saith the LORD of hosts." Malachi 3:8 – 12

"Give, and it shall be given unto you; good measure, pressed down, and shaken together, and running over, shall men give into your bosom. For with the same measure that ye mete (use) withal it shall be measured to you again." Luke 6:38

[6] "But this I say, He which soweth sparingly shall reap also sparingly; and he which soweth bountifully shall reap also bountifully. [7] Every man according as he purposeth in his heart, so let him give; not grudgingly, or of necessity: for God loveth a cheerful giver." II Corinth. 9:6,7

[9] "Honour the LORD with thy substance (possessions), and with the firstfruits of all thine increase: [10] So shall thy barns be filled with plenty, and thy presses (vats) shall burst out with new wine." Prov.3:9,10

Session #2

Scripture Reading – Proverbs 23:7, Romans 12:1,2   Renew the Mind

Session & Action Exercises #2   **Casting Down Imaginations**

2 Corinth. 10:3-5 "For though we walk in the flesh, we do not war after the flesh; (For the **weapons** of our warfare are not carnal, but **mighty through God** to the pulling down of strong holds;) **Casting down imaginations,** and every high thing that exalteth itself against the knowledge of God, and bringing into captivity every thought to the obedience of Christ;

Your imagination has divine power. It's a weapon against the enemy. But he works to turn your own weapon on you for evil.

<u>imagination</u> is formed from <u>image</u>

image – a reproduction or imitation of the form of a person or thing. A mental picture of something not actually present: IMPRESSION.

imagination – **1:** the act or power of forming a mental image of something not present to the senses never before wholly perceived in reality   2 : **a**   creative ability   **3 a** : a creation of the mind; *esp* : an idealized or poetic creation **b** : fanciful or empty assumption

We are created in the image of God; therefore, Satan will work against the power of our imagination to keep us from being transformed into that image. He works to redirect the power of our imagination (creative ability) to produce negative things rather than good things. He put wrong thoughts in our mind, so we can imagine negative things about ourselves and what our present and future holds for us. In **Prov. 23:7a** *it is written*, "For as he thinketh in his heart, so is he:"

He plays on our mind with fancy and futile assumptions. He desires to keep us seeing ourselves small and not accomplishing great things. He uses our imagination to keep us impoverish in every area of life. We can see his full work of redirected imagination among the pessimist.

Use your imagination for good. Think good thoughts about yourself. Erase the negative pictures from your mind and picture/visualize God bringing to pass in your life the promises written in His Word. When you visualize the promises of God, it gives you hope and that hope can turn into something miraculous.

For instance, visualize *Luke 6:38;* see people giving to you.
"**Give, and it shall be given unto you; good measure, pressed down, and shaken together, and running over, shall men give into your bosom. For with the same measure that ye mete withal it shall be measured to you again.**" Luke 6:38

Picture God bringing to pass what he said in His word for every area of your life.

We have to cast down negative images with the Word of God and see images of health in every area of our life for which he has made provision.

impoverish – to make poor. to deprive of strength, richness, or fertility by depleting or draining of something essential.

pessimism – an inclination to emphasize adverse aspects, conditions, and possibilities or to expect the worst possible outcome. the doctrine that reality is essentially evil. the doctrine that evil overbalances happiness in life.

<u>Helpful scriptures</u>
Beloved, I wish above all things that thou mayest prosper and be in health, even as though soul prosper." **III John 2** (picture prosperity in all that concerns you)

"For I know the thoughts that I think toward you, saith the LORD, thoughts of peace, and not of evil, to give you an expected end (a future and a hope)." **Jeremiah 29:11** (picture the LORD thinking good thoughts of you)

"…: and with his stripes we are healed." **Isaiah 53:5b** (see yourself healed)

Exercise { Close your eyes and picture (see) that Scripture manifested in your life}

Read Psalm 18:32-42 and picture yourself as a mighty warrior equipped by God.

Session #3

Scripture Reading – Colossians 2: 11 – 23 Freed To Serve Christ

Session & Action Exercise #3   Pulling down/Demolishing Strongholds

2 Corinth. 10:3-5 "For though we walk in the flesh, we do not war after the flesh; (For the **weapons** of our warfare are not carnal, but **mighty through God** to the **pulling down of strong holds**;) Casting down imaginations, and every high thing that exalteth itself against the knowledge of God, and bringing into captivity every thought to the obedience of Christ;

stronghold – a fortified place. a place of security or survival. a place dominated by a particular group or marked by a particular characteristic.

strong - having or marked by great physical power. having moral or intellectual power.

Strong may imply power derived from muscular vigor, large size, structural soundness, intellectual or spiritual resources.

hold (n) – stronghold. confinement, custody. prison. the act or the manner of holding or grasping : GRIP. a nonphysical bond that attaches, restrains, or constrains or by which something is affected, controlled, or dominated [has lost its ~ on the broad public].

hold (vb) – to have possession or ownership of or have at one's disposal. to keep under restraint. to have or maintain in the grasp. to prevent from leaving or getting away. to restrain as or as if a captive. to think in a particular way. to maintain occupation, control, or defense of. to maintain position : refuse to give up ground. to maintain a grasp on something : remain fastened to something.

hold back – to hinder the progress or achievement of : RESTRAIN.
hold down – something used to fasten an object in place. an act of holding down. LIMIT.

Listed are some strongholds that believers have to be aware of.

<u>Judgmental spirits</u>

Satan will use people's thoughts & opinions about you (good or bad) to put you in a stronghold. We can be vulnerable to this because we want folks to think well of us and like us. We have to be careful in this area because we don't want to find ourselves in a stronghold to their thoughts and opinions (judging). We want to avoid that trap. We don't want our life centered on judgmental spirits but on God. A person can never be truly happy when they are living their life to please people rather than God. God wants us to be joyful Christians serving him freely!

"Who are thou that judgest another man's servant? To his own master he standeth or falleth. Yea, he shall be holden up: for God is able to make him stand." Romans 14:4

How does a person get free from people's thoughts and opinions (judgmental spirit)?

Answer: Forsake being a people pleaser and become a lover of God.

[37] "He that loveth father or mother more than me is not worthy of me: and he that loveth son or daughter more than me is not worthy of me. [38] And he that taketh not his cross, and followeth after me, is not worthy of me. [39] He that findeth his life shall lose it: and he that loseth his life for my sake shall find it." **Matt. 10:37-39**

[23] And he said to them all, "If any man will come after me, let him deny himself, and take up his cross daily, and follow me. [24] "For whosoever will save his life shall lose it: but whosoever will lose his life for my sake, the same shall save it. [25] For whosoever shall be ashamed of me and of my words, of him shall the Son of man be ashamed, when he shall come in his own glory, and in his Father's, and of the holy angels. **Luke 9:23-26**

Master and slave mentality
If we seek to please people, we will find ourselves in a stronghold to their thoughts and words. We do not have to buy good treatment from them by becoming their subjects. When we are in a stronghold to their thoughts and words, we are their slaves. We have voluntarily given them the control over us. Jesus said we couldn't serve two masters. What they think about you controls our life. It's not your will be done, but their will. They doesn't give you a choice. Even God gives you a choice: Him or Satan, Heaven or Hell.

Condemnation spirits
condemn – [more at damn] to declare to reprehensible, wrong, or evil *usu.* after weighing evidence and without reservation. to pronounce guilty. to adjudge unfit for use or consumption. *Syn* see CRITICIZE

condemnation – the act of judicially condemning. the state of being condemned. a reason for condemning.

Condemnation in a person toward another person springs from measuring a person by their standard – that person not being good enough, not bowing down to them, not doing or saying what they want you to say or do, not being perfect, etc. Their goal is to make you feel inferior to them.

If God have not condemned you, neither shall they. The Word says in Romans 8:1 *"There is therefore now no condemnation to them which are in Christ Jesus, who walk not after the flesh, but after the Spirit."*

We may find ourselves saying and doing what people like rather than what God said to say and do. No matter what we say, every word is judged against us. We may try to find a better way to say something, but it still doesn't help. Their attitude and feelings toward us still doesn't change. We have to come to the conclusion that the problem is not with us, but them. They have to get free from their own devilish stronghold of condemnation. We have to work on ours and pray they will see to work on their's.

All this is a plan of the enemy to cause you to fall. Demolish the stronghold! Don't let their thoughts about you be your downfall, for that is the goal of the enemy. Yes, the devil sets goals and they are not pretty ones. You may not win them over, so in Love for them rise above their level and move forward (advance).

And Elijah came unto all the people, and said, **"How long halt ye (will you falter) between two opinions? If the LORD be God, follow him: but if Baal, then follow him. And the people answered him not a word." I Kings 18:21**

If the LORD be God, follow him: but if people, then follow them.

If there is condemnation in you toward another person, then sin is in you. You need to repent and the spirit of condemnation needs to be demolished with the weapon(s) of God.

<u>Witchcraft</u>
We should not allow people to bring us under their controlling power (aware or unaware): that's witchcraft.

witchcraft – an irresistible influence or fascination : ENCHANTMENT. the use of sorcery or magic. communication with the devil or with a familiar spirit.

When not allowing other to bring us under their control, let us make sure we do not allow our loving and submissive spirit to be damaged by opening ourselves us to be fertile ground for the enemy's seed of condemnation, rebellion, animosity, bad attitude, coldness, etc.

Exercise 1{Demolishing Strongholds through the weapon of Express/Verbal Authority}

Satan, It is written, "There is no condemnation to those who are in Christ Jesus. If Jesus has not condemned them, then who am I to condemn them? I will not join with you any longer in this evil spirit of condemnation of God's people or property; now be gone! He died so that they will be free from condemnation and so that I will be free from condemnation. And whom the Son has set free is free indeed! In Jesus' name. Amen.

Note: There are many sins a person can be in a stronghold to, but our weapons are mighty through God to demolish them. [lust, greed, pride, self-righteous, addictions, etc.]

There are also spiritual, mental, emotional, physical, and financial strongholds.

Session #4a

Scripture Reading – Luke 13:10 – 17   Christ Heals the Crippled Woman

Session & Action Exercises   #4a Casting out Demons/Devils/Evil Spirits

Matt. 16:19 "And I will give unto thee the **keys of the kingdom of heaven**: and whatsoever thou shalt bind on earth shall be bound in heaven: and whatsoever thou shalt loose on earth shall be loose in heaven."

keys of the kingdom of heaven [scriptures, revelation, knowledge, authority, power]

Mark 3:27 "No man can enter into a strong man's house, and spoil his goods, except he will first bind the strong man; and then he will spoil his house."

To bind is to prohibit
To loose is to permit

prohibit – to forbid by authority. to prevent from doing something .
Syn see FORBID
bind – a position or situation in which one is hampered, constrained, or prevented from free movement or action. **b :** to confine, restrain, or restrict as if with bonds **d :** to constrain with legal authority.
permit – (vb) **1 :** to consent to expressly or formally **2 :** to give leave: AUTHORIZE
permit – (n) **2 :** PERMISSION
loose – **2 a :** free from a state of confinement, restraint, or obligation

:and whatsoever thou shalt bind [by the words of thy mouth {believing}] on earth shall be bound in heaven [angels with bind on your behalf]

: and whatsoever thou shall loose [by the words of thy mouth {believing}] on earth shall be loose in heaven [angles will be released/sent to minister on your behalf].

Demons Have to Be Force To Leave

The Lord has given us power to drive out demons. But some demons are not going to give up their home so easily. There are times when spiritual, mental, and physical endurance and stamina are necessary. Sometimes it will take a team of Believers. Some spirits may drain you spiritually, mentally, & physically before they even think about leaving. If there is a problem, the devil will enhance it. They will not leave out by our power or might, but by the power of the Holy Spirit and in Jesus' name.

If we are not spiritual, mental, and physical fit to drive them out, we should at least get them to shut up or be quiet. Jesus told demons on several occasions to keep silent.

Here is a command to use in binding and loosing --

Satan/Devil I bind you in the name of Jesus, and by the power of the Holy Spirit, you foul spirit of _____, come out in the name of Jesus!

Cancer dry up and wither away.
Ears hear.
Eyes see.
Mind and body, be calm.

Exercise {Practice casting out these demons using the above command or cast it out of you if one is present [You can use an item for this exercise, such as a stuffed animal]}

cancer, deafness, tinnitus, blindness, fear, anxiety

Session #4b

Scripture Reading – Luke 10: 17–24   Believers' Authority through Jesus' Name

<u>**Session & Action Exercises #4b**</u>   **Spiritual Authority**

Demons

Ephesians 6:12 "For our struggle is not against flesh and blood, but against **the rulers**, against **the authorities**, against **the powers** of this dark world and against the **spiritual forces of evil in the heavenly realms.**

"Wherein in time past ye walked according to the course of this world, according to **the prince of the power of the air,** the (demonic) spirit that now worketh in the children of disobedience:" **Ephesians 2:2**

[the prince of the power of the air (exercising his ability and activities in a realm in the atmosphere)]

There are levels of ranks or classes among Satan's demons. But we still have authority over each rank or class in the Name and Authority of Jesus.

Luke 10:19 "Behold, I give unto you power to tread on serpents and scorpions, and over all the power of the enemy; and nothing shall by any means hurt you."

Angels

"Are they not all ministering spirits, sent forth to minister for them who shall be heirs of salvation." Heb. 1:14

[20] Bless the LORD, ye his angels, that excel in strength, that do his commandments, hearkening unto the voice of his word."

[21] Bless ye the LORD, all ye his hosts; ye ministers of his, that do his pleasure. [22] Bless the LORD, all his works (workers) in all places of his dominion: bless the LORD, O my soul." Psalm 103:20 – 22

[20] Behold, I send an Angel before thee, to keep thee in the way, and to bring thee into the place which I have prepared. [28] And I will send hornets (angels) before thee, which shall drive out the Hivite, the Canaanite, and the Hittite, from before thee." Exodus 23:20,28

"The angel of the LORD encampeth round about them that fear him, and delivereth them." Psalm 34:7

God have given angels charge over us to fight against the devil and his host on our behalf. The angles help keep balance between good and evil in the world. Unseen by our natural eyes in the spirit realm they are at work keeping things in order. They assist each other in meeting our needs. They are workers defending, protecting, rebuilding and restoring lives. They are at work to bring sinners to Christ and plays a part in our spiritual growth. They are reapers that gathers harvest into our lives from the seeds we plant in faith in what ever form: prayer, time, money, faithfulness and obedience in the Word, gifts/talents, kindness, love, giving of ourselves, etc. They minister on our behalf fulfilling the Word of God according to our lifestyle in Christ Jesus. They appropriate the promises of God to the faithful.

Spiritual Warfare (Mental Torments/Ills)

Taking authority though binding and loosing (releasing) over your children. [Bind demons and release angels]

Have your child invite Jesus into their heart so they can become heir of the promises. Then you can claim the right to the promises for them and declare the Word over them.

<u>Below are some scriptures you can use :</u>

[6]"And I will give peace in the land, and ye shall lie down, and none shall make you afraid: and I will rid evil beasts (eliminate wild beasts) out of the land, neither shall the sword go through your land. [7] And ye shall chase your enemies, and they shall fall before you by the sword." Lev. 26:6,7

[24] "Shall the prey be taken from the mighty, or the lawful captive (the captive of the righteous) delivered? [25] But thus saith the LORD. Even the captives of the mighty shall be taken away, and the prey of the terrible shall be delivered: for I will contend with him that contendeth with thee, and I will save thy children." Isaiah 49:24,25

[13] And all thy children shall be taught of the LORD; and great shall be the peace of thy children [17] No weapon that is formed against thee shall prosper; and every tongue that shall rise against thee in judgment thou shalt condemn. This is the heritage of the servants of the LORD, and their righteousness is of (from) me, saith the LORD." Isaiah 54:13,17

Additional scriptures:

[17] " The righteous cry, and the LORD heareth, and delivereth them out of all their troubles. [19] Many are the afflictions of the righteous: but the LORD delivereth him out of them all."   Psalm 34:17,19

[20] " He sent his word, and healed them and delivered them from their destructions [29] He maketh the storm a calm, so that the waves thereof are still."   Psalm107:20,29

[39] "And he arose, and rebuked the wind, and said unto the sea, Peace, be still. And the wind ceased, and there were a great calm." Mark 4:39

[36] " If the Son therefore shall make you free, ye shall be free indeed." John 8:36

[8] "I will both lay me down **in peace**, and sleep: for thou, LORD, only makest me dwell in safety." Psalm 4:8

[7] "For God hath not given us the spirit of fear, but of power, and of love, and of a **sound mind**." 2 Tim. 1:7

[22] "But the fruit of the Spirit is love, joy**, peace**, longsuffering, gentleness (kindness), goodness, faith (faithfulness), [23] Meekness, temperance (self-control):against such there is no law." Gal. 5:22

[16] "For who hath known the mind of the Lord, that he may instruct him**? But we have the mind of Christ."**

Exercise { Taking Authority over mental torments/ills. Lay your hand on the child's head and say something to this effect:}

Satan, in the name of Jesus and by the power of the Holy Spirit I bind your evil rulers, authorities, and powers from influencing my kids behavior. My child is an heir to the promises. It is written, "Great shall be the peace of thy children. And no weapon that is formed against them shall prosper." I command you to leave. Today angels are listening to the Word that I speak and they are imparting to them soundness of mind and good judgment. Thank you, Jesus. Let your mind be in them. Amen

Satan, in the name of Jesus and by the power of the Holy Spirit I bind your evil rulers, authorities, and powers from tormenting my _____ mind. The Lord said in Isaiah 49:25 "Even the captives of the mighty shall be taken away, and the prey of the terrible shall be delivered: for I will contend with him that contendeth with thee, and I will save thy children. I command you to leave. Angelic rulers, powers, and authorities are released now to bring peace and soundness of mind to them. Lord, let your mind be in them. Thank you, Jesus. Amen

Satan, in the name of Jesus and by the power of the Holy Spirit I bind your evil power of ADD from tormenting my _____ mind. I command you to leave. The Lord said in Lev. 26:6,7 "And I will give peace in the land, and ye shall lie down, and none shall make you afraid: and I will rid evil beasts (eliminate wild beasts) out of the land, neither shall the sword go through your land. ⁷ And ye shall chase your enemies, and they shall fall before you by the sword." Angelic rulers, powers, and authorities are driving away evil spirits now and they are imparting peace and soundness in their mind. Lord, let your mind be in them. Thank you, Jesus. Amen

Spiritual Warfare in the Financial Realm:
Angels on Assignments

Give seeds of money against these financial spirits (poverty, lack, and debt). If you do not have money to give, then whatever you do have to give, give it regularly. Most of all give in faith believing and expecting God to turn things around.

Release angels to fight on your behalf by quoting scriptures that opposes these financial spirits. We don't have control over the angles as far as owning them, but we can control what they do by what we do and say. It is written in Psalm 103:20 that angels hearken (listen) to the voice of his Word. We give voice to the Word when we speak it. When we speak it, the angels hear it and are released to fulfill God's promises in our lives.

> "Bless the LORD, ye his angels, that excel in strength, that do his commandments, hearkening unto the voice of his word." Psalm 103:20

> Angels are ministering spirits (Psalm 103:20). They are camped around us. (Psalm 34:7)

Lord, I ask that you send your angel to gather my harvest into my life from the seeds that I have sown. Your word says, such and such, so I'm expecting an angel to bring it to exist, to make it happen. Thank you Jesus. Amen

Satan, in the Authority and power of Jesus' name I rebuke your spirit of lack and I demand that you take your hand of my financial wealth. I release the Word of God against you. It is written, "The Lord is my shepherd and I shall not lack, wealth and riches are in the house of the righteous, and my God shall supply all my need according to his riches in glory by Christ Jesus. Furthermore, I am redeemed from the curse of the law of poverty. There is neither shortage nor struggle. All my bills are paid and debts canceled. I'm a tither and giver; God is causing people to give to me. Hallelujah and thank you Jesus! Amen!

<u>Below are some scriptures you can use :</u>

"But my God shall supply all your need according to his riches in glory by Christ Jesus." Phil. 4:19

"Christ has redeemed us from the curse of the law.." Gal.3:13

"In the house of the righteous is much treasure:…" Prov.15:6

"Wealth and riches shall be in his house: and his righteousness endureth for ever." Ps. 112:3

"Honour the LORD with thy substance, and with the firstfruits of all thine increase: so shall thy barns be filled with plenty, and thy presses (vats) shall burst out with new wine." Prov.3:9,10

"Give, and it shall be given unto you; good measure, pressed down, and shaken together, and running over, shall men give into your bosom. For with the same measure that ye mete withal it shall be measured to you again." Luke 6:38

"Bring ye all the tithes into the storehouse, that there may be meat in mine house, and prove me now herewith, saith the LORD of hosts, if I will not open you the windows of heaven, and pour you out a blessing, that there shall not be room enough to receive it. " And I will rebuke the devourer for your sakes, and he shall not destroy the fruits of your ground; neither shall your vine cast her fruit before the time in the field, saith the LORD of hosts." Mal. 3:10,11

Session #5

Scripture Reading – 2 Corinthians 4:1–7 The Light of The Gospel

Session & Action Exercises #5   The Suppressor of Light

^{V4} "The god of this age has blinded the minds of unbelievers, **so that they cannot see the light of the gospel of the glory of Christ**, who is the image of God. ⁶ For God, who said , "**Let light shine out of darkness**," made his light to shine in our hearts to give us **the light of the knowledge of the glory of God** in the face of Christ.

suppress – to put down by authority or force: SUBDUE. to keep from public knowledge: as, **a:** to keep secret **b**: to stop or prohibit the publication or revelation of. to exclude from consciousness. to inhibit the growth or development of: STUNT.

suppressor – one that suppresses.

suppression – an act or instance of suppressing : the state of being suppressed.

distort – to twist out of the true meaning or proportion *[~ the fa*cts]. To twist out of a natural, normal, or original shape or condition. (PERVERT- to twist the meaning or sense of)

distortion – the quality or state of being distorted : a product of distortion: as **a:** a lack of proportionality in an image resulting from defects in the optical system **b**: falsified reproduction of an audio or video signal caused by change in the wave form of the original signal.

Satan has blind the eyes of the world from seeing the light of the gospel of the glory of Christ so that they will not be saved. Since believers have received this <u>light of truth,</u> the devil now works to prevent them from receiving further Truth.

Satan forms weapons against believers to block the light of the truth from shining in our minds. He uses these weapons to hinder revelation knowledge from being made plain. He uses them to distort our discernment what the Spirit is revealing to us. He seeks to blind us from insight into the Truth. He uses them to cause the light to become scramble. All this is done in an attempt to discourage believers from growth. He does not have power over the light, but he can cause the message to become distorted by you.

Satan aims his weapons at the head: Weapons that suppresses your perception to blind your mind. Satan head weapons: headaches/tension headaches, irritability, mental anxiety, mental fatigue, and others. These weapons prevent you from concentrating and perceiving what the Spirit is saying.

You know that God has shined light on a Word, but you cannot discern or perceive it clearly to give proper words to it because a weapon of the enemy is distorting it. An important thing not to do is try to mentally figure it out. When we try to mentally figure it out, we may downgrade or distort the message. We start putting our own words to it, rather than the Spirit words. Our best course of action is to commune with the Lord on what was revealed: what he said will agree with the written Word.

Exercise 1 {Subdue the enemy of blindness – spiritual}
1st Lay hand on your head and rebuke the devil
2nd Command the head infirmity to be gone
3rd Bind the suppressing spirit
4th Command the mind to be clear or free from distortion
5th Ask the Lord to shine the light again

Suggested command and prayer:

Satan, in Jesus' name I rebuke you from my mind. You always seek to destroy the work of God. It is written, "No weapon that is formed against me shall prosper." I call your headache weapon destroyed and I bind your suppressing spirit in the power of the Holy Spirit.

I am headache free and distortion free and I discern without error. Lord Jesus, Let the light of truth, knowledge, and revelation shine out of darkness. Thank you, Jesus. Amen.

"No weapon that is formed against thee shall prosper; and every tongue that shall rise against thee in judgment thou shalt condemn. This is the heritage of the servants of the LORD, and their righteousness is of me, saith the LORD." Isaiah 54:17

Exercise 2 {Subdue the enemy of blindness – physical}
Read Mark 8:22-26

1st Lay hand on eyes and bind the spirit of blindness
2nd Command the eyes to see

If you had to minister healing to a blind person and she/he did not received sight the first time you laid hands on him/her. What would you do? What did Jesus do?

Note: In administering healing to the eyes, you should ask the person what eye problem they have and speak against the problem. (glaucoma, cataracts, infection, detached retina, astigmatism, crossed eyes, walleyed, etc.)

Session #6A

Scripture Reading –I Corinthians 13: 1 – 3 Faith Works By Love

<u>Session & Action Exercises #6A</u>   The Power of Faith [Moving mountains]

Mark 11:22-24 *"Have faith in God,"* Jesus answered. I tell you the truth, if anyone says to this mountain, 'Go throw yourself into the sea,' and does not doubt in his heart but believes that what he says will happen, it will be done for him. Therefore I tell you, whatever you ask for in prayer, believe that you have received it, and it will be yours."

Matt: 17:20 "If ye have faith as a grain of mustard seed, ye shall say unto this mountain, Remove hence to yonder place; and it shall remove; and nothing shall be impossible unto you."

Matt 21:21,22 Jesus answered and said unto them, "Verily I say unto you, If ye have faith, and doubt not, ye shall not only do this which is done to the fig tree, but also if ye shall say unto this mountain, Be thou removed, and be thou cast into the sea; it shall be done.[22]And all things, whatsoever ye shall ask in prayer, believing, ye shall receive."

Luke 17:6 "And the Lord said, If ye had faith as a grain of mustard seed, ye might say unto this sycamine tree, Be thou plucked up by the root, and be thou planted in the sea: and it should obey you."

Action Exercises #6A

Command a stone to move

Command electric currents to flow through a dead battery or wire

If the rock moves or the electric current flows, it's not magic it's the power of faith.

Suggested command
>Stone/Rock according to the Word of God I can speak to you in faith and you must move. So in Jesus' name I say to you, "Be thou removed, and be thou cast into the sea."

>Dead battery I command electric currents to flow through you in Jesus' name.

Command mountains of debt to dry up or move. Command something/s to dry up and wither away in your life in Jesus' name.

Note: Mountains don't float they sink to the bottom.

Session #6B

Scripture Reading – James 5:17,18 The Miracle of Rain
{Read the full account in I Kings 18:41 – 46}

<u>**Session & Action Exercises #6b**</u>   **Greater Works/Created Miracles**

John 14:12 "Verily, verily, I say unto you, He that believeth on me, the works that I do shall he do also; and greater works than these shall he do; because I go unto my Father."

Romans 4:17 "As it is written, I HAVE MADE THEE A FATHER OF MANY NATIONS, before him whom he believed, even God, who quickeneth the dead, and calleth those things which be not as though they were."

Luke 3:5,6 "Every valley shall be filled, and every mountain and hill shall be brought low; and the crooked shall be make straight, and the rough ways shall be made smooth; ^{6} And all flesh shall see the salvation of God."

Jesus said we would do greater work because He goes to His Father. When Jesus returned to Heaven, He sent the Holy Spirit to Earth. He lives in us and he works through us to perform many wonderful works. Though faith and the power of the Holy Spirit we can call those things that's not as though they were. We can call things into existence. With God all things are possible to them that believe. Don't limit what God can do through you. The Holy Spirit is still creating miracles today!

<u>Action Exercises #6B</u>
{Call those things that are dead back to life. Call body parts into existence. Call things that the world say can't happen, won't happen, or impossible}

You can say something like this—

Dream in Jesus' name I call life back into you. I say rise up in me and live!

Rebuke the spirit of death and call life.
Rebuke the thief and command a seven-fold return.
Rebuke the destroyer and call restoration.

Lord, by the power of thy Holy Spirit let there be a new leg, arm, thumb, heart, etc. You said we would do greater works because you go to your Father. Thank you, Jesus for granting this miracle. Amen.

Luke 3:5,6 "Every valley shall be filled, and every mountain and hill shall be brought low; and the crooked shall be make straight, and the rough ways shall be made smooth; ⁶ And all flesh shall see the salvation of God."

"Every valley shall be filled,...

If you know some things that need to be filled, such as a cavity: call it filled. Place your hand on your jaw/cheek area and declare, Lord your word said or It is written, "Every valley shall be filled, so cavity in Jesus' name be filled. Thank you, Jesus.

- Call a hole in the heart close or call a new heart into existence.

- Call the valley in your life to be filled with good things.

...and every mountain and hill shall be brought low,...

If you know some things (tangible and intangible) that needs to be brought low, such as; hemorrhoids, bumps or lumps on the body, lay your hand or touch it with your finger and declare, Lord your word said or It is written, "every mountain and hill shall be brought low. Fluid dry up and bump be flat in Jesus' name. Thank you, Jesus.

Touch the hemorrhoids and say, It is written, "every mountain and hill shall be brought low."

Rebuke inflammation and irritation. Say to the fluid, "you dry up and tissue you shrink in Jesus' name. Thank you, Jesus. Amen.

; and the crooked shall be make straight..

- Crooked spine or other crooked things

Touch the top of your spine and say, Lord your word said or It is written, the crooked shall be made straight. So spine you be straight in Jesus'name. Thank you, Jesus. Amen

, and the rough ways shall be made smooth,..

- Skin problems, ie. Rashes

Place your hand on the rash and say, Lord your word said or It is written, "the rough ways shall be made smooth, so skin be smooth in Jesus' name. Thank you, Jesus. Amen

[6] And all flesh shall see the salvation of God."

- Need an overall/overhaul: Head to toe

Place your hand on your head and say, Lord your word said or It is written, "all flesh shall see the salvation of God, so from head to toe I am renewed inside and out. My spirit, soul, and body are made whole. In Jesus' name. Thank you, Jesus. Amen

Note: If you don't see results right away it is okay to speak to the infirmity several times a day. When you take medicine you are instructed to take it once a day or several times a day for a period of time. The Word is health (medicine) to all your flesh according to Prov. 4:20-22

Remember by His stripes you are healed. Isaiah 53:5

Note: Whether you say, <u>Lord it is written or your word said</u> – they are equivalent.

FYI:
Lay hand suddenly on no man [I Tim 5:22]
If you know or not sure whether the infirmity is contagious, use a prayer cloth. (See Ways to Heal)

Prayer; Combined With Ways To Heal

Ways to Heal – Faith

[34] "And he said unto her, Daughter, thy faith hath made thee whole; go in peace, and be whole of thy plague." Mark 5:34

[29] "Then touched he their eyes, saying, According to your faith be it unto you. [30] And their eyes were opened;" Matt. 9:29,30

Ways to Heal – the Word

[20] "He sent his word, and healed them, and delivered them from their destructions." Ps. 107:20

[8] "The centurion answered and said, Lord, I am not worthy that thou shouldest come under my roof: but speak the word only, and my servant shall be healed." Matt. 8:8

Ways To Heal – Laying On Hands

"He said to them, "Go into all the world and preach the good news to all creation. Whoever believes and is baptized will be saved, but whoever does not believe will be condemned. And these signs will accompany those who believe: **In my name they will drive out demons**; they will speak in new tongues; they will pick up snakes with their hands; and when they drink deadly poison, it will not hurt them at all; **they will place their hands on sick people, and they will get well."
Mark 16:13-18**

Ways To Heal – Anointing Oil

Anoint – to rub or smear with oil or an oily substance

Mark 6: 7-13

[13] "And they cast out many devils (demons), and anointed with oil many that were sick, and healed them."

James 5:13 – 15

[14] "Is any sick among you? Let him call for the elders of the church; and let them pray over him, anointing him with oil in the name of the Lord:"

Ex. 40:9 – 11 Moses was command by God to anoint the Tabernacle and everything in it. [So we anoint our houses and goods according to this Scripture]

Whatever you anoint, say, " I anoint _____ in Jesus' name.
Use anointing oil to bless your house and goods. Rebuke evil spirits from your house and call goods spirits and things to come in according to the Scripture.

A Way To Get Your Healing – Intercessory Prayer

> James 5: 16 – 18
> <u>Praying for others shows love and un-selfishness</u>. If you know someone who is going through the same thing you are going through, pray for them before you pray for yourself.

Ways to Heal – Touching and Agreeing

> [19] "Again I say unto you, that if two of you shall agree on earth as touching any thing that they shall ask, it shall be done for them of my Father which is in Heaven. [20] For where two or three are gathered together in my name, there am I in the midst of them." Matt. 18:19,20

Ways to Heal – Prayer Cloths (A point of contact)

[11] "And God wrought special (unusual) miracles by the hands of Paul: [12] So that from his body were brought unto the sick handkerchiefs or aprons, and the diseases departed from them, and the evil spirits went out of them." Acts 19:11,12

A point of contact for releasing your faith. The anointing is transferrable.

The woman with the issue of blood said, " If I may but touch his garment, I shall be whole." Matt. 9;20,21

There were others who touched his hem. Some got healed. Some didn't. The different was the one essential element that we all must have: Faith. Matt.14:35,36

Ways to Deliverance/Heal – Music

The power of music --
"As they began to sing and praise, the Lord set ambushes against the men of Ammon, Moab, and Mount Seir who were invading Judah, and they were defeated." 2 Chr. 20:22

I Samuel 16:14 – 23 [READ]
When David played his harp, evil spirits left Saul.

CONCLUSION

⁴"And my speech and my preaching was not with enticing (persuasive) words of man's wisdom, but in <u>demonstration of the Spirit and of power</u>; ⁵ that your <u>faith</u> should not stand (be) in the wisdom of men, but in the <u>power of God</u>."   I Corinth. 2:4,5

³⁵ Cast not away therefore your confidence, which hath great recompense of reward."   Heb.10:35

Barbara A. Perry is a teacher of the Word of God and a Christian writer. She is the founder and senior pastor of Spirit of Prevailing Faith in Aiken, South Carolina. She has been a pastor for over 20 years. She is sole proprietor of Garden 33 Publisher. She is married to Jimmie Perry.  She has two daughters: Alice and Samantha and three grandchildren: Da'Shawn, Samara, and Natalie.

www.ingramcontent.com/pod-product-compliance
Lightning Source LLC
Chambersburg PA
CBHW020024050426
42450CB00005B/625